Practice Tests

for

Baron
ESSENTIALS OF PSYCHOLOGY

Second Edition

Thomas T. Jackson
Fort Hays State University

Allyn and Bacon
Boston   London   Toronto   Sydney   Tokyo   Singapore

Copyright © 1999 by Allyn & Bacon
A Viacom Company
160 Gould Street
Needham Heights, Massachusetts 02194-2130

Internet: www.abacon.com
America Online: keyword: College Online

All rights reserved. No part of the material protected by this copyright notice
may be reproduced or utilized in any form or by any means, electronic or
mechanical, including photocopying, recording, or by any information
storage and retrieval system, without the written permission of the copyright owner.

ISBN 0-205-28847-2

Printed in the United States of America

10 9 8 7 6 5 4   03 02 01 00

TABLE OF CONTENTS

Introduction

Chapter 1:	Practice Test 1	1
	Practice Test 2	3
Chapter 2:	Practice Test 1	5
	Practice Test 2	7
Chapter 3:	Practice Test 1	9
	Practice Test 2	11
Chapter 4:	Practice Test 1	13
	Practice Test 2	15
Chapter 5:	Practice Test 1	17
	Practice Test 2	19
Chapter 6:	Practice Test 1	21
	Practice Test 2	23
Chapter 7:	Practice Test 1	25
	Practice Test 2	27
Chapter 8:	Practice Test 1	29
	Practice Test 2	31
Chapter 9:	Practice Test 1	33
	Practice Test 2	35
Chapter 10:	Practice Test 1	37
	Practice Test 2	39
Chapter 11:	Practice Test 1	41
	Practice Test 2	43
Chapter 12:	Practice Test 1	45
	Practice Test 2	47
Chapter 13:	Practice Test 1	49
	Practice Test 2	51
Chapter 14:	Practice Test 1	53
	Practice Test 2	55
Answer Keys		57

INTRODUCTION

These practice tests were prepared for use with Robert A. Baron's *Essentials of Psychology* (2th Edition). Each chapter has two practice tests covering the material in the chapter. Each test has 15 multiple choice questions with four alternatives for each question. The questions are similar to those that may be given to you in tests for this particular course. Answer keys for all tests are in the back of this booklet. The answer keys consist of the correct answer for each question, plus the page number where that material is located in the chapter.

For your convenience in looking up answers and page numbers, each practice test has a heading that tells you which test you are taking, and the headings match the headings on the answer keys. In addition, each question is numbered with the chapter number along with a number between 1 and 15. For example, Item 11.4 from Practice Test 1 is from Chapter 11 and is the fourth question from that chapter. There is a range of difficulty for the questions, and some of the questions are fairly challenging, so for each question, select the best answer for that question.

A suggestion for using these practice tests would be for you to study the textbook chapter and then take one of the practice tests to see how well you grasped the material. After taking the test, look up the answers in the answer key and check to see how you scored. Write down the page numbers of any questions you missed and look up that material in the textbook and make sure that you understand the material. Then, take the second practice test and see how you scored. Again, look up any material that you are not quite sure of, using the page numbers in the answer key.

These practice tests can help you become familiar with the material in the textbook, as well as help you become familiar with the type of questions asked over the material. Such familiarity should be of benefit to you as you progress through the course.

Good fortune to you in your psychology course.

Tom Jackson, PhD
Fort Hays State University

PRACTICE TESTS

Chapter 1 - Psychology: A Science ... and a Perspective

Practice Test 1

1.1 The individual usually credited with selling his colleagues on the idea of an independent science of psychology is
   a. Gustav Fechner.
   b. Hermann von Helmholtz.
   c. Johannes Muller.
   d. Wilhelm Wundt.

1.2 Psychologists who felt that psychology should study only observable activities were the
   a. functionalists.
   b. structuralists.
   c. behaviorists.
   d. experimentalists.

1.3 Psychologists who try to understand how we think and remember are taking a _____ perspective.
   a. physiological
   b. psychodynamic
   c. social-cultural
   d. cognitive

1.4 The relatively recent emphasis in psychology on the multicultural perspective is partly a result of which social trend?
   a. Improvements in health care mean that there are more and more elderly Americans.
   b. An increasingly technological society makes higher education more and more important.
   c. Widespread immigration is bringing together people with differing ethnic backgrounds.
   d. Television has created a generation of children who think visually and often can't read.

1.5 Suppose Ralph tries out a new intelligence test, but the first two or three people who use it complain that it is too hard. If Ralph concludes from this information that the test is bad, it would violate the principle of scientific
   a. open-mindedness.
   b. functionality.
   c. accuracy.
   d. empiricism.

1.6 The main purpose of theories is to
   a. explain.
   b. postdict.
   c. evaluate.
   d. summarize.

1.7 The common sense approach to psychology is often characterized by
   a. objective evaluations.
   b. contradictory statements.
   c. direct experimentation.
   d. systematic observation.

1.8 Which of the following statements best reflects an attitude of critical thinking with respect to the report of a research project?
   a. I don't care what they say, I won't believe it.
   b. Of course, I've always known that was true.
   c. I really like what these people are saying.
   d. I wonder how they measured that variable.

1.9 Freud based many of his ideas about personality on extensive interviews with his clients. He had them tell him about their lives, especially their early childhood experiences. Freud's method of obtaining information is referred to as
   a. naturalistic observation.
   b. systematic desensitization.
   c. case method.
   d. meta-analysis.

1.10 Your high school guidance counselor sends you a questionnaire to complete about many of your high school experiences. The counselor indicates that the questionnaire has been sent to all graduates within the last ten years. In all likelihood, your counselor is using which of the following methods?
   a. survey method
   b. double-blind method
   c. naturalistic observation method
   d. case method

1.11 As the strength of a negative correlation increases, the ability to predict the value of one variable from another
   a. increases.
   b. decreases.
   c. stays the same.
   d. cannot be determined.

1.12 In an experiment, the factor that is varied is called the _____ variable.
   a. control
   b. dependent
   c. independent
   d. stimulus

1.13 If the likelihood by chance of obtained results is less than or equal to .05, the results are described as being
   a. meaningful.
   b. significant.
   c. meaningless.
   d. not interpretable.

1.14 Giving a participant full information about all aspects of an experiment after the participant has fulfilled his or her role in an experiment is referred to as
   a. confounding.
   b. deception.
   c. informed consent.
   d. debriefing.

1.15 Which of these scenes reflects the most common type of ethical problem that occurs in the practice of psychology?
   a. A researcher deliberately falsifies the results of an experiment.
   b. A doctor prescribes medication that addicts a client.
   c. A therapist learns that a client has committed a crime.
   d. A counselor falls in love with a client.

PRACTICE TESTS

Practice Test 2

1.1 Observable behavior is to conscious behavior as
   a. structuralism is to behaviorism.
   b. structuralism is to psychoanalysis.
   c. behaviorism is to psychoanalysis.
   d. behaviorism is to structuralism.

1.2 The _____ was the result of combining new research techniques with a growing interest in mental processes.
   a. cognitive revolution
   b. artistic revolution
   c. experimental revolution
   d. behavioral revolution

1.3 Your textbook defines "Psychology" as
   a. the investigation of conscious and unconscious processes.
   b. the science of behavior and cognitive processes.
   c. the scientific study of human behavior.
   d. the study of the mind.

1.4 Which of the following is not one of the grand issues of psychology?
   a. nature vs. nurture
   b. reality vs. irreality
   c. stability vs. change
   d. rationality vs. irrationality

1.5 An individual who is employed as a human factors psychologist would be interested in
   a. evaluating the situations that create difficulties for humans.
   b. assessing human behavior from a trait perspective.
   c. designing equipment that is easy and convenient for humans to use.
   d. measuring the factors that influence human behavior.

1.6 An important sources of ideas for studies in psychology is
   a. literature.
   b. theory.
   c. common sense.
   d. mathematics.

1.7 Which of the following indicates the strongest relationship?
   a. -.39
   b. +.39
   c. +.65
   d. -.73

1.8 In an experiment, the variable that is manipulated by the experimenter is called the
   a. independent variable.
   b. dependent variable.
   c. control variable.
   d. confound variable.

1.9 The most important characteristic of an experiment is that
   a. measurements are made under controlled conditions.
   b. causal relationships can be established.
   c. predictions can be made accurately.
   d. control factors are negligible.

1.10 In an experiment, all participants in a noisy condition are tested on Mondays and those in the no noise condition are tested on Wednesdays. The noise and day of week variables are
   a. implicated.
   b. confounded.
   c. contrived.
   d. interactive.

1.11 An experiment in which neither the participants nor the researchers know the hypothesis under investigation is using
   a. an experimenter effects procedure.
   b. a confound control procedure.
   c. a double blind procedure.
   d. a random assignment procedure.

1.12 Because it is often necessary to conceal certain aspects of an experiment, experimental psychologists may use the technique of
   a. deception.
   b. projection.
   c. subliminal stimulation.
   d. conversion.

1.13 One important principle surrounding the use of deception in an experiment is that all participants should be _____ after they have completed the experiment.
   a. informed of their rights
   b. thanked
   c. debriefed
   d. rewarded

1.14 Lisa is a therapist and has received information from a client about a crime that was committed. Lisa now has a conflict of
   a. confidentiality.
   b. security.
   c. relationship.
   d. interest.

1.15 Research indicates that _____ learning is more efficient than _____ learning.
   a. contiguous, continuous
   b. cognitive, conative
   c. crammed, spaced
   d. spaced, crammed

PRACTICE TESTS

Chapter 2 - Biological Bases of Behavior: A Look Beneath the Surface

Practice Test 1

2.1 The three basic parts of the neuron are
   a. vesicles, gray matter, and the synapse.
   b. telodendria, nodes of Ranvier, and synaptic terminals.
   c. cell body, axon, and dendrites.
   d. myelin sheath, cell body, and dendrites.

2.2 A sheath of fatty material that covers the axon of many nerve cells and plays a role in the transmission of information is called
   a. glial.
   b. myelin.
   c. acetylcholine.
   d. ion membrane.

2.3 The stage at which the neuron has a slightly negative charge is called the
   a. dynamic state.
   b. steady-state stage.
   c. action potential.
   d. resting potential.

2.4 The electrical signal that travels down the axon of a neuron toward the next cell is called the
   a. action potential.
   b. glial message.
   c. threshold.
   d. myelin sheath.

2.5 Since neurons only fire when the right pattern of information reaches them, they can be conceived of as
   a. small modular transmitters.
   b. tiny decision-making mechanisms.
   c. tiny modular receivers.
   d. small information mechanisms.

2.6 Drugs seem to affect our behavior and cognitive processes primarily by changing
   a. thalamic structures.
   b. synaptic transmission.
   c. the shape of the axons.
   d. the number of axon terminals.

2.7 Which of the following is not one of the functions of the spinal cord?
   a. regulates reflexes
   b. conducts information from receptors to the brain
   c. conducts information from the brain to the muscles
   d. connects the central nervous system to the involuntary muscles

2.8 A procedure for measuring the electrical activity of the entire brain is called
   a. superconducting quantum interference device or SQUID.
   b. positron emission tomography or PET.
   c. high-tech snooper or HTS.
   d. electroencephalography or EEG.

2.9 Which of the following structures regulates the autonomic nervous system?
   a. thalamus
   b. cerebellum
   c. hypothalamus
   d. medulla

2.10 The frontal lobes, the parietal lobes, the temporal lobes, and the occipital lobes together make up the
   a. cerebellum.
   b. hypothalamus.
   c. medulla.
   d. cerebral hemispheres.

2.11 The lobe concerned with vision is
   a. occipital.
   b. temporal.
   c. frontal.
   d. parietal.

2.12 Research has found that during the making of a decision, the _____ hemisphere is active; once the decision is made, the _____ hemisphere is active.
   a. left; left
   b. left; right
   c. right; right
   d. right; left

2.13 The brain structure that regulates many basic body functions is the _____. It regulates these functions through the action of the "master gland," the _____.
   a. left hemisphere; thyroid
   b. right hemisphere; parathyroid
   c. cerebellum; adrenal gland
   d. hypothalamus; pituitary

2.14 Which statement is not true about genes?
   a. They contain thousands of segments of DNA.
   b. Most human traits are determined by more than one gene.
   c. Genes influence behavior directly.
   d. There is evidence for genetic involvement in a variety of physical and mental disorders.

2.15 Most cells contain _____ chromosomes.
   a. 23
   b. 46
   c. 31
   d. 43

PRACTICE TESTS

Practice Test 2

2.1 The part of the neuron that conducts action potentials toward the cell body is called the
   a. dendrite.
   b. axon.
   c. synapse.
   d. myelin.

2.2 The "nodes of Ranvier" are the
   a. gaps between axons and dendrites of connecting neurons.
   b. gaps in the myelinated sheath of an axon.
   c. gaps in the synaptic vesicles.
   d. gaps that occur in the ion channels of a neuron.

2.3 Structures located in the axon terminals that contain chemicals used in nerve cell communication are called
   a. neuron containers.
   b. chemical vesicles.
   c. synaptic vesicles.
   d. ion pouches.

2.4 One of the most important neurotransmitters that affects muscular movements is
   a. norepinephrine.
   b. serotonin.
   c. dopamine.
   d. acetylcholine.

2.5 The nervous system is viewed as composed of two major parts, the _____ and the _____.
   a. peripheral nervous system, autonomic nervous system
   b. parasympathetic nervous system, central nervous system
   c. central nervous system, peripheral nervous system
   d. autonomic nervous system, parasympathetic nervous system

2.6 The part of the peripheral nervous system that connects the central nervous system to the voluntary muscles is the _____ nervous system.
   a. central
   b. sympathetic
   c. parasympathetic
   d. somatic

2.7 Results of PET scans suggest that as we become more familiar with a task or problem, neural activity is
   a. always processed in the same area as it was first processed.
   b. processed first on the left side and then on the right side of the brain.
   c. delegated to different areas of the brain as a result of hypothalamic activity.
   d. shifted from the cortex to more automatic brain regions.

2.8 The cerebellum is that part of the brain that is most involved in the
   a. regulation of sleep.
   b. regulation of basic motor activities.
   c. regulation of hunger.
   d. regulation of core brain temperature.

2.9 Damage to the thalamus is most likely to cause
   a. clumsiness and lack of coordination.
   b. difficulty seeing or hearing.
   c. an inability to stay awake.
   d. complete loss of appetite.

2.10 Which one of the following is not one of the lobes in the cerebral cortex?
   a. frontal lobe
   b. partial lobe
   c. temporal lobe
   d. occipital lobe

2.11 According to the Wernicke-Geschwind theory, which of the following areas would disrupt speech comprehension if damaged?
   a. Broca's area
   b. medulla oblongata
   c. left frontal lobe
   d. Wernicke's area

2.12 The corpus callosum is
   a. the sheath covering over the cerebral cortex.
   b. a connecting fiber between the temporal lobe and the occipital lobe.
   c. a band of nerve fibers connecting the two hemispheres of the brain.
   d. the integrating fibers from the brain to the heart.

2.13 Phenylketonuria (PKU), a genetically based disorder, leading to mental retardation and other disorders can be regulated by
   a. surgery.
   b. genetic manipulation.
   c. diet.
   d. exercise.

2.14 In an investigation of the nature-nurture controversy, Lykken and his colleagues (1993), found
   a. greater similarity of occupational interests among identical twins (raised together and raised apart) than nonidentical twins.
   b. less similarity of occupational interests among identical twins raised apart than nonidentical twins.
   c. greater similarity of occupational interests among nonidentical twins raised together than identical twins raised apart.
   d. greater similarity of occupational interests among nonidentical twins raised apart than identical twins raised apart.

2.15 A critical ingredient of successful treatment of TBI involves
   a. how often the intervention is applied.
   b. when the intervention is applied.
   c. by whom the intervention is applied.
   d. if the intervention is cognitively oriented.

PRACTICE TESTS

Chapter 3 - Sensation and Perception: Making Contact with the World around Us

Practice Test 1

3.1   The definition of perception involves
   a.   transduction.
   b.   interpretation.
   c.   simplicity.
   d.   direct sensation.

3.2   The absolute threshold is usually defined as the magnitude of physical energy one can detect _____ % of the time.
   a.   10
   b.   30
   c.   50
   d.   70

3.3   The sensory receptors in the eye are found in the
   a.   retina.
   b.   cochlea.
   c.   ganglion cells.
   d.   cornea.

3.4   The visual feature most important for your dog to catch frisbees in the air is
   a.   angular velocity.
   b.   static visual acuity.
   c.   dynamic visual acuity.
   d.   saccadic movements.

3.5   The theory that holds that there are six cells that play a role in color vision is
   a.   trichromatic theory.
   b.   opponent process theory.
   c.   signal detection theory.
   d.   dark adaptation theory.

3.6   Which of the following theories suggests that sounds of different pitch cause different rates of neural firing?
   a.   frequency theory
   b.   place theory
   c.   opponent process theory
   d.   field theory

3.7   When a person's culture emphasizes the stoical acceptance of pain, a person is likely to respond by
   a.   overacting and responding excessively to pain.
   b.   enjoying pain, and inflicting it on others.
   c.   becoming able to tolerate high levels of pain silently.
   d.   making no change; this will not affect one's perception of pain.

3.8   The theory put forth to explain how we detect odors based on different molecular shapes is the
   a.   opponent process theory.
   b.   stereochemical theory.
   c.   electromagnetic theory.
   d.   malodorous detection theory.

3.9 The sense that gives us information about the location of our body parts with respect to each other and allows us to perform movements is called
   a. vestibular.
   b. prosopagnosia.
   c. kinesthesia.
   d. gustation.

3.10 Basic ways in which we group items together perceptually are known as the
   a. proximity principle.
   b. good continuation rule.
   c. closure laws.
   d. laws of grouping.

3.11 The ability to perceive stability in the face of change defines
   a. perceptual illusions.
   b. perceptual constancies.
   c. closure orientation.
   d. laws of grouping.

3.12 Exact representation of stimuli stored in memory are called
   a. features.
   b. binocular cues.
   c. prototypes.
   d. templates.

3.13 Blakemore and Cooper (1970) demonstrated that raising kittens in a restricted visual environment seemed to cause permanent deficits in the kitten's later perceptions. These results support the notion that some aspects of perception are
   a. determined by nature.
   b. modified by phi stimuli.
   c. learned.
   d. innate.

3.14 Overt transmission of thoughts from one person to another is
   a. telepathy.
   b. clairvoyance.
   c. precognition.
   d. psychokinesis.

3.15 The use of personal stereo headsets at high volume increases the probability of the occurrence of
   a. auditory latitude.
   b. ocular latitude.
   c. tinnitus.
   d. nystagmus.

PRACTICE TESTS

Practice Test 2

3.1 The definition of sensation involves
    a. knowledge.
    b. interpretation.
    c. simplicity.
    d. the senses.

3.2 An experimenter has you compare the temperature of water in two different containers. She asks you if they feel the same or different. She is probably trying to determine your
    a. subliminal threshold.
    b. absolute threshold.
    c. difference threshold.
    d. frequency threshold.

3.3 A "just noticeable difference" is
    a. the smallest amount of a neuronal stimulus that is detectable.
    b. the smallest amount of change in a physical stimulus that is detectable.
    c. the smallest amount of change in a neuronal stimulus that is detectable.
    d. the smallest amount of a physical stimulus that is detectable.

3.4 At the point of exit of the optic nerve from the eyeball, there
    a. are no visual receptors.
    b. is a concentration of visual receptors.
    c. is a concentration of rods.
    d. is a concentration of cones.

3.5 The saccadic movements of poor readers
    a. are smooth.
    b. are jerky.
    c. are long.
    d. are circular.

3.6 The greater the _____, the _____ the pitch.
    a. amplitude, higher
    b. frequency, lower
    c. amplitude, lower
    d. frequency, higher

3.7 Which part of the body contains the most skin receptors for touch?
    a. The bottom of the foot.
    b. The front of the knee.
    c. The tips of the fingers.
    d. The forehead.

3.8 The sensation of a dull, throbbing pain can get through to the brain, while quick, sharp pain cannot, according to
    a. gate-control theory.
    b. hydraulic action theory.
    c. temporal matching theory.
    d. pain-recognition theory.

3.9 The nose has over 10 million receptor cells for smell in the
    a. vestibular sacs.
    b. olfactory epithelium.
    c. semicircular canals.
    d. basilar membrane.

3.10 The way we select, organize, and interpret sensory input is termed
 a. perception.
 b. sensation.
 c. cognition.
 d. conation.

3.11 The tendency to shift the focus of our attention toward meaningful, unattended information is known as the
 a. risky-shift effect.
 b. cocktail party phenomenon.
 c. template matching effect.
 d. prototype matching phenomenon.

3.12 The tendency to perceive objects as whole entities, even when parts may be missing, is known as the
 a. law of similarity.
 b. law of proximity.
 c. law of closure.
 d. law of continuation.

3.13 Theories that propose that perceptions may be determined by our expectations are
 a. prototype theories.
 b. top-down theories.
 c. bottom-up theories.
 d. feature theories.

3.14 Retinal disparity occurs because
 a. there are more rods than cones.
 b. we have a discrepancy in the fovea of the eyeball.
 c. our eyes see slightly different views of objects in space.
 d. our retinas have distended areas that cause blurred vision.

3.15 Perception without a basis in perception is known as
 a. alternate sensory perception.
 b. ultrasensory perception.
 c. subconscious perception.
 d. extrasensory perception.

PRACTICE TESTS

Chapter 4 - States of Consciousness

Practice Test 1

4.1 A hormone that seems to influence circadian rhythm is
   a. adrenalin.
   b. endorphins.
   c. testosterone.
   d. melatonin.

4.2 Research on automatic processing suggests that
   a. it requires a lot of attention.
   b. it is more flexible than controlled processing.
   c. it is slower than controlled processing.
   d. it requires little conscious awareness.

4.3 Most people spend more time _____ than they spend in any other activity.
   a. problem solving
   b. daydreaming
   c. fantasizing
   d. sleeping

4.4 During REM sleep, a person is usually
   a. sleeping lightly and very easy to wake up.
   b. sleeping deeply and displaying delta waves.
   c. displaying sleep spindles and K complexes.
   d. experiencing dreams and lack of bodily activity.

4.5 Reading something pleasant or taking a warm bath before going to bed and establishing a regular sleep routine are recommended for treating
   a. night terrors.
   b. insomnia.
   c. somnambulism.
   d. narcolepsy.

4.6 A disturbance that involves stopping of breathing while sleeping is
   a. hypersomnia.
   b. apnea.
   c. night terrors.
   d. somnambulism.

4.7 During which stage of sleep do dreams usually occur?
   a. During REM sleep
   b. During Stage 1 sleep
   c. During Stage 2 sleep
   d. During Stage 3 sleep

4.8 If you wake up disturbed from a dream where you were engaging in a bad habit that you are trying to change, e.g, biting your nails, you probably experienced
   a. automatic processing.
   b. dreams of absent-minded transgression (DAMIT dreams).
   c. neodissociation dreams.
   d. narcoleptic fantasies.

4.9 Which of the following emphasizes the relationship between the hypnotist and the hypnotized person, where the hypnotized person engages in activities believed to happen in the context of hypnotism?
   a. social-cognitive
   b. neodissociation
   c. automatic processing
   d. social-dissociative

4.10 If someone takes a drug out of a strong desire to feel its effects and a fear of facing life without it, the person has developed
   a. a physiological dependence on the drug.
   b. a psychological dependence on the drug.
   c. a medical condition for which the drug is the treatment.
   d. a hallucinogenic factor in the use of the drug.

4.11 People take drugs to reduce anxiety generated by unconscious conflicts according to which of the following perspectives?
   a. psychodynamic
   b. cognitive
   c. learning
   d. social

4.12 Drugs that reduce both behavioral output and activity in the central nervous system are classified as
   a. narcotics.
   b. depressants.
   c. opiates.
   d. psychedelics.

4.13 Which of the following, if ingested, is likely to result in increased blood pressure, heart rate, and respiration?
   a. only cocaine
   b. only amphetamines
   c. only caffeine
   d. cocaine, amphetamines, and caffeine

4.14 Which of the following is not a correct statement about opiates?
   a. Heroin is an opiate.
   b. The pain reducing ability of the user may be reduced.
   c. Their use produces dramatic slowing of bodily functions.
   d. They may cause an increase in endorphins.

4.15 A technique performed to produce altered states of consciousness in which awareness of and contact with the external world is reduced is called
   a. yoga analysis.
   b. meditation.
   c. synesthesia.
   d. regression.

PRACTICE TESTS

Practice Test 2

4.1 Research on circadian rhythms uses the _____ approach.
   a. EEG
   b. diary
   c. cross-sectional
   d. longitudinal

4.2 Imaginary scenes and events that occur while an individual is awake are called
   a. fantasies.
   b. controlled processing.
   c. daydreams.
   d. automatic processing.

4.3 Sexual fantasies are common for both men and women, and are a problem only when the fantasies
   a. focus on inappropriate partners.
   b. occur several times during the day.
   c. occur with the same theme.
   d. focus on the same individual every time.

4.4 Respiration, muscle tone, heart rate, and blood pressure are behaviors typically used to study
   a. aphasia.
   b. sleep.
   c. controlled processing.
   d. automatic processing.

4.5 Research indicates that the
   a. total amount of Stage 3 sleep increases with age.
   b. total amount of Stage 1 sleep increases with age.
   c. total amount of sleep decreases with age.
   d. total amount of sleep increases with age.

4.6 The strongest result of depriving people of REM sleep is that the people begin to show
   a. significant memory losses for their daily experiences.
   b. major mood changes, including depression.
   c. increased risks for infectious diseases.
   d. more REM sleep the next few nights.

4.7 An individual who tends to fall asleep during the midst of waking activities may be suffering from
   a. insomnia.
   b. hypersonmia.
   c. apnea.
   d. narcolepsy.

4.8 An individual who is susceptible to hypnotism has many specific characteristics, among them being
   a. low in the trait of absorption.
   b. high on the likelihood of experiencing stronger dissociative experiences.
   c. low on expectations of outcome.
   d. high on the social trait of independence.

4.9 Research examining the effects of hypnotism on sensation and perception indicates that hypnotism
   a. can completely block our sensory systems.
   b. can mimic the effects of most hallucinogens.
   c. alters the subject's report of the sensory experience and not the actual experience.
   d. selectively inhibits the neural sensory systems of the brain but not the cognitive cortical areas.

4.10 Compounds that have the ability to change the functioning of biological systems are called
   a. drugs.
   b. cognates.
   c. biogenerators.
   d. dissociatives.

4.11 Which of the following depress activity in the nervous system causing a reduction in mental alertness and also produce feelings of relaxation and euphoria?
   a. amphetamines
   b. nicotine
   c. LSD
   d. barbiturates

4.12 One of the characteristics of barbiturates is that they tend
   a. to increase Stage 1 sleep.
   b. to suppress REM sleep.
   c. to increase REM sleep.
   d. to suppress Stage 1 sleep

4.13 Drugs that alter sensory perception and are considered "mind expanding" are called
   a. peptides.
   b. barbiturates.
   c. psychedelics.
   d. hallucinogens.

4.14 One of the most dangerous aspects of LSD is that
   a. the effects are unpredictable.
   b. the effects are mostly negative.
   c. the effects are extreme.
   d. the effects are limiting.

4.15 Research indicates that during meditation an individual's
   a. oxygen intake increases.
   b. homeostasis is restored.
   c. REM increases.
   d. heartbeat may slow.

PRACTICE TESTS

Chapter 5 - Learning: How We're Changed by Experience

Practice Test 1

5.1 Learning how to throw a basketball as a result of watching games on television is an example of
   a. pseudolearning.
   b. classical conditioning.
   c. operant conditioning.
   d. observational learning.

5.2 When studying classical conditioning, subjects would often salivate at the sight of the pan where food was kept. In this case, salivating to the food is an example of
   a. an unconditioned stimulus.
   b. an unconditioned response.
   c. a conditioned stimulus.
   d. a conditioned response.

5.3 Simultaneous, trace, delayed, and backward conditioning are produced as a result of manipulating
   a. temporal arrangements between the CS and US.
   b. temporal arrangements between the CR and US.
   c. intensity of the US.
   d. intensity of the CS.

5.4 When the unconditioned stimulus no longer follows the conditioned stimulus, _____ occurs.
   a. spontaneous recovery
   b. extinction
   c. classical conditioning
   d. operant conditioning

5.5 Stimulus generalization
   a. is the tendency of stimuli dissimilar to the conditioned stimulus to produce conditioned responses.
   b. is identical to stimulus discrimination.
   c. is the tendency of stimuli similar to the conditioned stimulus to produce conditioned responses.
   d. occurs when the US and CS are no longer paired.

5.6 Conditioned taste aversions
   a. are easy to extinguish.
   b. require many CS-US pairings.
   c. are difficult to extinguish.
   d. occur with animals, but not with people.

5.7 Preventing conditioning to a neutral stimulus as a result of presenting this new neutral stimulus along with a previous unconditioned stimulus is called
   a. omission training.
   b. conditioning constraints.
   c. flooding.
   d. blocking.

5.8 Pairing saccharin-flavored water with injection of a substance known to raise the level of antibodies in rats' bodies later resulted in _____ after being again exposed to saccharin-flavored water.
   a. decreases in antibodies
   b. increases in antibodies
   c. increased liking for saccharin-flavored water
   d. aversion to saccharin-flavored water

5.9 Stimuli that strengthen responses related to their escape or avoidance are
   a. negative reinforcers.
   b. positive reinforcers.
   c. primary reinforcers.
   d. secondary reinforcers.

5.10 Animals that have been shaped to do unusual behavior may return to more natural behavior. This is called
   a. extinction.
   b. instinctive drift.
   c. acquisition.
   d. shaping.

5.11 The schedule of reinforcement that leads to low rates of responding immediately after the presentation of a reward, but a high rate of responding when the time for reward is near is called
   a. fixed ratio.
   b. fixed interval.
   c. variable ratio.
   d. variable interval.

5.12 Which of the following situations illustrates the function of stimulus control?
   a. Using proper table manners when eating with your family, but not when eating alone.
   b. Finding that one subject, French for example, is easier for you than Math.
   c. Working harder for partial rewards, such as paychecks, than for continuous rewards.
   d. Choosing a smaller reward that is immediately available over a larger one that is delayed.

5.13 A positive contrast effect occurs when subjects are shifted from a _____ to a _____ reward.
   a. small; large
   b. large; small
   c. positive; negative
   d. negative; positive

5.14 Albert Bandura analyzed the process of observational learning and concluded that four factors were important. These factors are
   a. the CS, the US, the CR, and the UR.
   b. stimulus generalization, discrimination, control, and reinforcement.
   c. attention, retention, production process, and motivation.
   d. classical, operant, motivational, and sensory conditioning.

5.15 If you were starting a weight loss program, which of the following principles of learning would be of most importance to you?
   a. spontaneous recovery
   b. blocking
   c. shaping
   d. extinction

PRACTICE TESTS

Practice Test 2

5.1 The type of conditioning that seems to play a role in strong fears, taste aversions, and even racial prejudices is
   a. observational learning.
   b. classical conditioning.
   c. operant conditioning.
   d. instrumental conditioning.

5.2 The process of acquisition
   a. proceeds slowly at first and then increases to maximum.
   b. proceeds slowly at first and then levels off.
   c. proceeds rapidly at first and then slows down.
   d. proceeds steadily to maximum.

5.3 Which of the following is not a factor that influences the acquisition of classical conditioning?
   a. timing
   b. familiarity
   c. intensity
   d. implosion

5.4 Research has indicated that there is increased neural firing in the _____ before the onset of the conditioned response.
   a. cerebellum
   b. temporal lobe
   c. thalamus
   d. cerebral cortex

5.5 Which of the following is false?
   a. Conditioning improves as the intensity of either the CS or US increases.
   b. All responses or associations are learned with equal ease.
   c. Taste aversion research shows that classical conditioning can occur with a relatively long interval between the CS and the US.
   d. Chaining usually begins by shaping the final response in a sequence of behaviors.

5.6 A progressive technique designed to replace anxiety with a relaxation response is called
   a. flooding.
   b. chaining.
   c. systematic desensitization.
   d. spontaneous recovery.

5.7 If someone tells you that you must eat all of your spinach before you get to read your favorite book, that person is using _____ to influence your behavior.
   a. the Garcia modification
   b. Skinnerian conditioning
   c. Pavlovian conditioning
   d. the Premack principle

5.8 Negative reinforcement is to punishment as
   a. response decrease is to response increase.
   b. response increase is to response decrease.
   c. response decrease is to response decrease.
   d. response increase is to response increase.

5.9 Operant conditioning involves
   a. the association between stimulus and response.
   b. the association between particular behaviors and their consequences.
   c. the association between acquisition and extinction.
   d. the association between responses.

5.10 Classes in college usually last for 50 minutes. Increased movement of students occurs toward the latter part of these periods. This increased movement is an example of a
   a. variable ratio schedule.
   b. fixed ratio schedule.
   c. variable interval schedule.
   d. fixed interval schedule.

5.11 Behaviors acquired by the _____ schedule are the most resistant to extinction.
   a. fixed interval
   b. fixed ratio
   c. variable interval
   d. variable ratio

5.12 Variable ratio schedules produce responses that are
   a. easy to extinction.
   b. resistant to extinction.
   c. usually fairly simple.
   d. usually fairly complex.

5.13 Research indicates that learned helplessness occurs partly because of
   a. our perception that we have lost control over our lives.
   b. our vicarious learning experiences.
   c. the emotion experienced when we have been frustrated reaching a goal.
   d. the cognition that occurs when a goal is blocked.

5.14 In a famous study by Tolman and Honzik (1930), rats apparently learned a maze without receiving any reinforcements. Tolman felt these results were evidence for the operation of
   a. instinctive drifting.
   b. biological constraints on learning.
   c. cognitive maps.
   d. vicarious learning.

5.15 The procedure of placing posters in three bathrooms sequentially in order to see the effect of these posters on graffiti is called
   a. sequential behavior design.
   b. random behavioral technique.
   c. multiple-baseline design.
   d. sequential baseline technique.

PRACTICE TESTS

Chapter 6 - Memory: Of Things Remembered ... and Forgotten

Practice Test 1

6.1 Locating and accessing specific information from memory when it is needed at later times is referred to as
   a. encoding.
   b. storage.
   c. retrieval.
   d. consolidation.

6.2 Memory that involves the total of each person's general, abstract knowledge about the world is called
   a. episodic memory.
   b. procedural memory.
   c. semantic memory.
   d. context-dependent memory.

6.3 The finding that memory span for immediate recall of lists of short words is greater than for lists of longer words is known as the
   a. word similarity effect.
   b. word length effect.
   c. word processing effect.
   d. word scanning effect.

6.4 The tip-of-the-tongue phenomenon occurs when we are trying to remember a fact, but instead we
   a. remember other information related to the fact.
   b. can't remember ever having known about it.
   c. remember the fact incorrectly.
   d. avoid the memory because it is too traumatic.

6.5 Which of the following requires the deepest level of processing when learning a list of words?
   a. repeating the information
   b. elaborative rehearsal
   c. determining whether two words rhyme
   d. judgements as to whether two words look alike

6.6 Ebbinghaus' early research indicated that forgetting is rapid at first and then slows down with the passage of time. This occurs most often when
   a. recognizing faces.
   b. retaining motor skills.
   c. remembering nonsense syllables.
   d. recalling life events.

6.7 Interference that occurs when information previously entered into memory interferes with the learning or storage of current information is called
   a. retroactive interference.
   b. proactive interference.
   c. prospective interference.
   d. elaborative interference.

6.8 People who challenge the accuracy of recovered memories of childhood abuse will often argue that
   a. there are too few of these cases to draw any conclusions.
   b. misguided therapists often push these ideas on their clients.
   c. people are faking these claims in an attempt to get money.
   d. people do not ever forget anything that happens to them.

6.9 According to Howe and Courage, the most likely explanation currently held for the inability to remember what happened during the first two or three years of life is
   a. insufficient brain mechanisms.
   b. the lack of language during this time period.
   c. the lack of self-concept during this time period.
   d. immaturity of the autonomic nervous system.

6.10 Compared with other memories, flashbulb memories are generally
   a. more semantic and less episodic.
   b. of events that happened long ago.
   c. not particularly accurate.
   d. extremely accurate.

6.11 Cognitive structures representing individuals' knowledge and assumptions about the world are called
   a. phonological loops.
   b. schemas.
   c. flashbulb memories.
   d. distortions.

6.12 Children from traditional societies many times perform more poorly on standardized memory tests than children from industrial societies. This finding emphasizes the fact that
   a. memory is not culturally contained.
   b. memory occurs against a cultural background.
   c. memory is culturally contained.
   d. memory occurs independent of cultural background.

6.13 Lisa cannot remember events that occurred immediately before her accident. She is suffering from
   a. retrograde amnesia.
   b. anterograde amnesia.
   c. proactive interference.
   d. retroactive interference.

6.14 Verbal is to nonverbal as
   a. episodic memory is to semantic memory.
   b. semantic memory is to episodic memory.
   c. explicit memory is to implicit memory.
   d. implicit memory is to explicit memory.

6.15 Possible mechanisms for storing memories in the brain include changes in
   a. the rate of production of specific neurotransmitter only.
   b. the structure of the neurons only.
   c. both the rate of production of specific neurotransmitters and the structure of the neurons.
   d. neither the rate of production of specific neurotransmitter nor the structure of the neurons.

PRACTICE TESTS

Practice Test 2

6.1 One of the earliest research findings in the area of memory and forgetting was by Ebbinghaus, who discovered that, using nonsense syllable, we
   a. forget material we have memorized very slowly at first, then forgetting levels off.
   b. forget material we have memorized quite rapidly at first, then forgetting slows down.
   c. forget material we have memorized very slowly at first, then forgetting increases.
   d. forget material at a steady rate.

6.2 Moving material from one memory system to another involves
   a. procedural categorizing processes.
   b. autonomic review processes.
   c. creative strategy processes.
   d. active control processes.

6.3 The major conclusions that have been gleaned from research on sensory memory are
   a. that sensory memory stores a limited amount of information for a long period of time.
   b. that sensory memory stores an impressive amount of information for a very short period of time.
   c. that sensory memory stores an impressive amount of information for a long period of time.
   d. that sensory memory stores a limited amount of information for a very short period of time.

6.4 The serial position curve reveals that material learned _____ of the list is remembered _____.
   a. at the end, worst
   b. at the beginning, worst
   c. in the middle, better
   d. in the middle, worst

6.5 Which of the following is used to keep information active in the short-term memory system?
   a. chunking
   b. semantic storage
   c. acoustical storage
   d. rehearsal

6.6 The process by which we locate material previously stored in memory is called
   a. searching.
   b. decoding.
   c. retrieval.
   d. encoding.

6.7 Stimuli that are associated with information stored in memory that help to evoke the memory when it cannot be recalled spontaneously are called
   a. retrieval cues.
   b. storage cues.
   c. shallow cues.
   d. deep cues.

6.8 Your mood at learning and recall is to the affective nature of the information is to
   a. mood-dependent memory, mood-affect memory.
   b. mood-dependent memory, mood-congruence effect.
   c. mood-congruence effect, mood-dependent memory.
   d. mood-affect memory, mood-congruence effect.

6.9 The _____ proposes that we forget material because of the passage of time.
   a. trace-decay hypothesis
   b. interference hypothesis
   c. time-delay hypothesis
   d. contiguity hypothesis

6.10 The initial stage of _____ seems to be involved in intentional forgetting.
   a. amnesia
   b. encoding
   c. retrieval
   d. storage

6.11 Questioning 60-year-old subjects about their college years by asking them the names of their teachers, courses they took, dorms they lived in, etc., is investigating
   a. prospective memory.
   b. autobiographical memory.
   c. phonological loop.
   d. method of loci.

6.12 Information that is _____ with well-developed schemas is encoded more readily than information that is _____ with our schemas.
   a. inconsistent; consistent
   b. not parallel; parallel
   c. consistent; inconsistent
   d. parallel; not parallel

6.13 A decrease in acetylcholine and increases in bundles of amyloid beta protein that may damage projections from nuclei in the basal forebrain to the hippocampus and cerebral cortex appears to be associated with
   a. flashbulb memories.
   b. Korsakoff's syndrome.
   c. Alzheimer's disorder.
   d. schizophrenia.

6.14 According to your textbook, damage to portions of the _____ produces deficits in implicit memory.
   a. occipital lobes
   b. temporal lobes
   c. frontal lobes
   d. hippocampus

6.15 The "first letter technique" involves
   a. using the first letters of items to construct an alphabetical listing of the items you wish to remember.
   b. using the first letters of items you wish to remember to make a word in that list.
   c. using the first letters of items in order to position them in locations easy to remember.
   d. making a sentence of the first letters of items in a list you want to remember.

PRACTICE TESTS

Chapter 7 - Cognition and Intelligence

Practice Test 1

7.1 Mental frameworks for categorizing diverse items as belonging together are
    a. hypotheses.
    b. ideas.
    c. prototypes.
    d. concepts.

7.2 Concepts can be represented as
    a. images.
    b. features.
    c. schemas.
    d. images, features, or schemas.

7.3 The main advantage of everyday reasoning, compared with formal reasoning, is that it can handle situations in which
    a. there is not enough information.
    b. the two propositions are reversed.
    c. it is guaranteed to give a correct answer.
    d. it is not influenced by cultural factors.

7.4 The anchoring-and-adjustment heuristic is strongly influenced by
    a. expected utility.
    b. base rates.
    c. a reference point.
    d. ambiguous information.

7.5 A disadvantage associated with using algorithms to solve problems is that algorithms often
    a. are too difficult to understand.
    b. produce contradictory solutions.
    c. are written for experts.
    d. are very inefficient.

7.6 The type of knowledge that involves understanding of the meaning of words is known as
    a. semantic development.
    b. phonological development.
    c. syntactical development.
    d. morphological development.

7.7 Artificial intelligence primarily involves the study of
    a. all animal communication.
    b. all primate communication.
    c. computer capabilities.
    d. analogies and algorithms.

7.8 Spearman felt that intelligence consisted of
    a. a single primary factor.
    b. multiple types of intelligence.
    c. a composite of seven primary mental abilities.
    d. culturally determined skills.

7.9 In Sternberg's triarchic theory, the ability to formulate new ideas or to combine seemingly unrelated facts is referred to as
    a. componential intelligence.
    b. experiential intelligence.
    c. contextual intelligence.
    d. crystallized intelligence.

7.10 A major problem with intelligence tests developed and adapted by Binet and Terman was that they paid relatively little attention to
    a. verbal abilities.
    b. memory abilities.
    c. age-related changes in intelligence.
    d. nonverbal abilities.

7.11 Assessment of similarity of scores over time is
    a. split-half reliability.
    b. test-retest reliability.
    c. split-half validity.
    d. test-retest validity.

7.12 The ability of a test to measure what it is supposed to measure is its
    a. predictive power.
    b. internal consistency.
    c. reliability.
    d. validity.

7.13 The more closely two people are related, the _____ their IQs.
    a. lower
    b. higher
    c. more similar
    d. more different

7.14 It seems likely that the worldwide increase in IQ scores is due to
    a. environmental factors.
    b. genetic factors.
    c. actual increase in intelligence.
    d. the ozone layer.

7.15 One part of emotional intelligence is being able to read the _____ of other people.
    a. cognitive overtones
    b. nonverbal cues
    c. potential conflicts
    d. overt emotions

PRACTICE TESTS

Practice Test 2

7.1 The clearest or best example of something is called
   a. a prototype.
   b. an exemplar.
   c. a concept.
   d. an denotation.

7.2 The confirmation bias implies that a person will
   a. attempt to confirm his or her conclusions by examining supportive and nonsupportive evidence.
   b. test his or her conclusions by examining primarily evidence that supports his or her initial view.
   c. act upon his or her biases without examining additional data.
   d. form a bias based upon limited evidence.

7.3 Lisa assumes that Ralph is intelligent because he wears glasses and is majoring in mathematics. Lisa is using one cognitive shortcut from a group of shortcuts known as
   a. cogitators.
   b. natural concepts.
   c. heuristics.
   d. processors.

7.4 According to the availability heuristic, the more easily we think of something, the more
   a. frequent we judge it to be.
   b. we like it.
   c. we dislike it.
   d. we understand it.

7.5 Ralph has been investing in the stock market, and in contrast to the rest of his friends, is losing a lot of money. Ralph continues to pour money into the market hoping he will make up his losses. Ralph has mortgaged his home to get additional money. Ralph's situation is a good example of
   a. affective decision making.
   b. diffusion of responsibility.
   c. a bear market.
   d. escalation of commitment.

7.6 An _____ is a rule that, if followed, guarantees a solution to a specific type of problem.
   a. exemplar
   b. algorithm
   c. heuristic
   d analogy

7.7 Our tendency to use things only in ways they have been used before is called
   a. mental set.
   b. metacognition.
   c. functional fixedness.
   d. perceptual set.

7.8 Which one of the following resources is not one of the resources listed by Lubart (1994) as being part of creativity?
   a. personality attributes
   b. analytical style
   c. intrinsic, task-focused motivation
   d. supportive environment

7.9 In order for a system of communication to be called a _____, the symbols must have meaning, the elements must be capable of being combined into sentences, and the meanings of these combinations must be independent of the particular settings in which they were developed.
   a. syntaxic system.
   b. semantic system
   c. phonological system
   d. language

7.10 The rules by which words are arranged into sentences in a specific language are called
   a. phonemes.
   b. morphemes.
   c. grammar.
   d. semantics.

7.11 It is difficult to determine if animals have the ability to combine a small number of words into unique combinations that convey a broad range of meaning, or _____.
   a. generativity
   b. creativity
   c. syntax
   d. functionality

7.12 According to the _____ theory of intelligence, there are seven primary mental abilities.
   a. Big Seven
   b. multifactor
   c. triarchic
   d. specific

7.13 According to Sternberg's triarchic theory, people who have practical sense have _____ intelligence.
   a. componential
   b. experiential
   c. contextual
   d. intuitive

7.14 One major problem with the use of group tests of intelligence is that they may be
   a. too difficult.
   b. culturally biased.
   c. too easy.
   d. not influenced by training.

7.15 The type of validity in which test scores are related to present behavior is
   a. content.
   b. predictive.
   c. concurrent.
   d. construct.

PRACTICE TESTS

Chapter 8 - Human Development

Practice Test 1

8.1 The face, arms, and legs are present by the _____ week of prenatal development.
   a. third
   b. fourth
   c. sixth
   d. eighth

8.2 The method of studying development that provides the clearest picture of the course of human development is the
   a. cross-sectional approach.
   b. longitudinal approach.
   c. longitudinal-sequential approach.
   d. experimental design.

8.3 Fitting experience into existing schema is known as
   a. preoperation.
   b. adaptation.
   c. accommodation.
   d. assimilation.

8.4 Research with children on the development of cognitive abilities has found that Piaget
   a. was essentially correct.
   b. underestimated cognitive abilities.
   c. overestimated cognitive abilities.
   d. overemphasized the role of sensory processes.

8.5 The information processing perspective of cognitive development
   a. seeks to map out the stages of development.
   b. seeks to understand how, and in what ways, children's capacity to process, store, retrieve, and actively manipulate information changes with age.
   c. proposes that private speech is egocentric.
   d. proposes that private speech represents attempts in social communication.

8.6 At the _____ level of moral development, we tend to judge morality in terms of what supports and preserves the social order.
   a. preconventional
   b. conventional
   c. postconventional
   d. abstract

8.7 What are psychologists measuring when they use the strange situation test?
   a. cognitive development
   b. conservation
   c. the appearance-reality distinction
   d. attachment to the mother

8.8 Harlow's research with monkeys showed that
   a. baby monkeys' attachments to their cloth mother could be reversed by rejection.
   b. the satisfaction provided by feeding is sufficient for attachment.
   c. the satisfaction provided by feeding is not sufficient for attachment.
   d. attachment in human infants is not the same as attachment in monkeys.

8.9 Different patterns of behavior that are expected of people because they are male or female are called
   a. gender stereotyping.
   b. sexism.
   c. sexual harassment.
   d. feminism.

8.10 Adolescents seek out novel and intense experiences, characteristic of individuals who are high on
   a. sensation seeking.
   b. peer pressure.
   c. drugs.
   d. invulnerability.

8.11 People usually become aware of declines in their physical systems
   a. in their twenties.
   b. in their thirties.
   c. in their forties.
   d. in their fifties.

8.12 The climacteric is associated with
   a. menopause.
   b. a person's ability to withstand intense heat.
   c. a person's ability to withstand intense cold.
   d. Erikson's third stage.

8.13 Fluid intelligence appears to _____ after the early twenties. Crystallized intelligence appears to _____ across the lifespan.
   a. increase; remain constant
   b. increase; decrease
   c. decrease; remain constant
   d. decrease; increase

8.14 The importance of free radicals in aging is emphasized by which of the following theories of aging?
   a. wear-and-tear theory.
   b. genetic theory.
   c. homeostatic theory.
   d. social theory.

8.15 According to Kubler-Ross, the first stage of the dying process is
   a. denial.
   b. anger.
   c. depression.
   d. bargaining.

PRACTICE TESTS

Practice Test 2

8.1 Factors in the environment that harm the developing fetus are known as
   a. teleomeres.
   b. teratogens.
   c. free radicals.
   d. collagens.

8.2 The fetal disorder that may involve retarded growth, irritability, and hyperactivity is associated with maternal
   a. alcohol consumption.
   b. caffeine intake.
   c. illegal drug use.
   d. smoking.

8.3 Meltzoff and his colleagues (1997), in a study concerned with infant behavior, found that 15 day old newborns were quite capable of
   a. directed voice patterns.
   b. indicating facial recognition.
   c. imitation.
   d. focused orientation.

8.4 Longitudinal research involves
   a. studying different people for an extended period of time.
   b. studying different people for a specified time period.
   c. studying the same people for a specified time period.
   d. studying the same people for an extended period of time.

8.5 Piaget believed that children engaged in the process of _____, which involved constructing mental representations of the world through direct interaction with it.
   a. adaptation
   b. assimilation
   c. accommodation
   d. conservation

8.6 According to Piaget, cognitive development involves interplay between _____ and _____.
   a. sensation and cognition.
   b. the id and the ego.
   c. assimilation and accommodation.
   d. emotion and motivation.

8.7 The proposal that changes in the ability of children to perform cognitive tasks results from changes in their ability to block out distractors and focus attention is most consistent with _____ view of development.
   a. Piaget's
   b. Vygotsky's
   c. the psychodynamic
   d. the information processing

8.8 Once children develop understanding of their own conscious processes, they have acquired
   a. variacognition.
   b. metacognition.
   c. unicognition.
   d. bilateral cognition.

8.9 An individual who judges whether an act is moral or not based on whether the act adheres to social rules or laws is at the _____ level of moral development.
   a. preconventional
   b. conventional
   c. postconventional
   d. metaconventional

8.10 Research indicates that there are gender differences in the area of psychological adjustment, with females twice as likely to suffer from some form of
   a. anxiety disorder.
   b. phobia.
   c. hysteria.
   d. depression.

8.11 According to Erikson's theory, the most important internal crisis faced by adolescents concerns resolving
   a. competence versus inferiority.
   b. initiative versus guilt.
   c. sexuality versus sexual confusion.
   d. identity versus role confusion.

8.12 Adolescents who are raised in harmful environments yet overcome these disadvantages and achieve healthy development have
   a. behavioral ebullience.
   b. cognitive accommodation.
   c. resilience in development.
   d. adolescent recklessness.

8.13 Aging is a continuous process that begins _____ in life. This process proceeds _____ at first.
   a. late; slowly
   b. early; slowly
   c. late; rapidly
   d. early; rapidly

8.14 When studying the long-term memory, young people seem to have the advantage of being able to _____ more meaningless material.
   a. reconstruct
   b. recognize
   c. redintegrate
   d. recall

8.15 The majority of people report having relatively high levels of personal happiness, or
   a. subjective well-being.
   b. resilience in development.
   c. connotative functionality.
   d. individualistic integrity.

PRACTICE TESTS

Chapter 9 - Motivation and Emotion

Practice Test 1

9.1 Motivational processes are used to explain behavior whenever
   a. there are apparent experiences, for example, prior rewards, that cause the behavior.
   b. the causes of the behavior are not readily discerned in the immediate surroundings.
   c. the behavior is lacking in energy, that is, its intensity is constant.
   d. emotions are influencing the behavior.

9.2 One major problem with instinct theory of motivation is that the existence of the instinct is inferred from
   a. physiological measures.
   b. observations.
   c. the behavior it was designed to explain.
   d. experimental analyses.

9.3 When studying behavior, Lisa likes to listen to classical music whereas her roommate insists that it be totally silent. The theory of motivation that can best explain these differences is
   a. arousal theory.
   b. drive theory.
   c. achievement theory.
   d. expectancy theory.

9.4 Which of the following theories of motivation include the role of incentives in producing motivation?
   a. expectancy theory
   b. arousal theory
   c. drive theory
   d. instinct theory

9.5 In Maslow's hierarchy of needs, deficiency needs are those that
   a. involve the respect and approval of others.
   b. must be satisfied before other needs emerge.
   c. develop in late childhood or adolescence.
   d. increase our overall level of arousal.

9.6 The fact that you always get popcorn and a soda when you go to the movies regardless of the time of day can best be explained on the basis of
   a. classical conditioning.
   b. cognitive expectancies.
   c. homeostasis.
   d. lipid detectors.

9.7 The Kinsey reports found that
   a. females were more sexually active than males.
   b. there was great individual variation in sexual behavior.
   c. only a minority of men and women have premarital sex.
   d. rates of homosexuality were higher than expected.

9.8 At times, people experience a desire to harm others when they have been prevented by these people from obtaining what they want. This is called the _____ hypothesis.
   a. frustration-aggression
   b. learning-catharsis
   c. frustration-catharsis
   d. catharsis-frustration

9.9 The desire to meet standards of excellence - to accomplish difficult tasks - is called
   a. achievement motivation.
   b. power motivation.
   c. excellence motivation.
   d. thematic motivation.

9.10 If we are going to reward people for intrinsically motivated activities, it is best if these rewards
   a. are a sign of recognition.
   b. are small.
   c. are unsatisfying.
   d. are external.

9.11 The primary difference between the Schachter-Singer theory and the older theories of emotion is that the Schachter-Singer theory emphasizes
   a. overt behaviors.
   b. conscious thoughts.
   c. physiological changes.
   d. subjective feelings.

9.12 According to the Opponent-process theory, if taking an exam makes you experience anxiety, when you finish the exam you will experience
   a. greater anxiety.
   b. depression.
   c. anger.
   d. relief.

9.13 Someone who spends an evening watching a Marx Brothers movie, a Naked Gun movie, and two hours of stand-up comedy is likely to show more than usual brain activity in
   a. the right cerebral hemisphere.
   b. the left cerebral hemisphere.
   c. the brain stem.
   d. the parasympathetic nervous system.

9.14 What is the effect of mood on interviewers' ratings of an applicant?
   a. Interviewers in a good mood give more critical ratings.
   b. Interviewers in a good mood give more positive ratings.
   c. Interviewers' mood only affects ratings when the mood is negative.
   d. Interviewers' mood is not related to ratings given applicants.

9.15 Which of the following behaviors is not an indicator of lying?
   a. The pitch of a person's voice often rises.
   b. The pupils of a person's eyes often become dilated.
   c. The ears of a person turn red.
   d. The facial expressions of a person are often exaggerated.

PRACTICE TESTS

Practice Test 2

9.1 Internal processes that activate, guide, and maintain behavior over time are know as
   a. reinforceement.
   b. motivation.
   c. needs.
   d. drives.

9.2 According to drive theory, behaviors will be repeated if they tend to
   a. increase drives.
   b. have no effect on drives.
   c. decrease drives.
   d. initiate drives.

9.3 The Yerkes-Dodson Law states that performance is often best when arousal is _____.
   a. controlled
   b. low
   c. high
   d. moderate

9.4 Which of the following is not a correct statement about Maslow's theory?
   a. Motives exist in a hierarchy.
   b. Motives at the bottom must be satisfied before those at the top.
   c. Deficiency needs include esteem needs.
   d. Self-actualization is a growth need.

9.5 Behavior is _____ by expectations of desired outcomes, and _____ by biologically based drives.
   a. pushed, pulled
   b. pulled, pushed
   c. reinforced, nonreinforced
   d. nonreinforced, reinforced

9.6 If sex hormones are present, sexual behavior occurs. When sex hormones are not present, sexual behavior does not occur. The presence of sex hormones produce
   a. satiation effects.
   b. arousal effects.
   c. activation effects.
   d. gonadatropic effects.

9.7 A refractory period is a time during which
   a. an orgasm is imminent.
   b. men cannot be sexually aroused.
   c. women can have multiple orgasms.
   d. the genitals become enlarged.

9.8 In a study on the response differences between males and females to sexual infidelity,
   a. younger males reported being more likely to respond with aggression.
   b. older males reported being more likely to respond with aggression.
   c. males reported being more likely to respond with aggression.
   d. females reported being more likely to respond with aggression.

9.9 Lisa goes to a psychologist's office and the psychologist asks for her responses to a set of ambiguous pictures. This psychologist is probably measuring _____ using the _____.
   a. achievement motivation, Rorschach Inkblot Test
   b. aggressive motivation, Rorschach Inkblot Test
   c. achievement motivation, TAT
   d. aggression motivation, TAT

9.10 Which of the following is not true of high achievement oriented individuals?
   a. high grades in school
   b. prefer difficult tasks
   c. success in running their own business
   d. rapid promotions.

9.11 Intrinsic motivation involves
   a. doing activities for the enjoyment the activities provide.
   b. doing activities for the external rewards provided.
   c. doing activities for the inherent goodness of the activities.
   d. doing activities because of their worth.

9.12 If you see a bear, run away from that bear, and then know fear, you have demonstrated the
   a. Cannon-Bard theory of motivation.
   b. James-Lange theory of motivation.
   c. Two-factor theory of motivation.
   d. Opponent-Process theory of motivation.

9.13 What are the two factors that determine a person's emotional experience according to the Schachter-Singer two-factor theory?
   a. intensity of affect and behavior being performed
   b. intensity of affect and whether the situation is positive or negative
   c. body gestures and transfer of excitation
   d. internal arousal and choice of label for this arousal based on external stimuli

9.14 In our culture, making a circle of one's thumb and forefinger represents "OK." Such a body movement is called a
   a. microexpression.
   b. gesture.
   c. macroexpression.
   d. posture.

9.15 One way in which cognition can affect emotions is through the activation of _____ with a strong affective component.
   a. contagions
   b. conations
   c. schemas
   d. consistencies

PRACTICE TESTS

37

Chapter 10 - Personality: Uniqueness and Consistency in the Behavior of Individuals

Practice Test 1

10.1 The part of the mind that contains the impulses of which we are not aware, according to Freud, is the
   a. conscious.
   b. preconscious.
   c. unconscious.
   d. subconscious.

10.2 According to Freud, the part of our personality that functions on the basis of the reality principle is the
   a. id.
   b. ego.
   c. superego.
   d. conscious.

10.3 A defense mechanism that channels unacceptable impulses into a socially acceptable action is called
   a. reaction formation.
   b. repression.
   c. regression.
   d. sublimation.

10.4 Fixation at the _____ stage, stemming from traumatic toilet training experiences, may result in individuals who are excessively orderly.
   a. latency
   b. genital
   c. oral
   d. anal

10.5 The neo-Freudian who proposed the existence of the collective unconscious was
   a. Adler.
   b. Jung.
   c. Horney.
   d. Fromm.

10.6 The text indicates that one important result of the struggle between the neo-Freudians over Freud's theory was that they
   a. disproved all the important features of Freud's theory.
   b. demonstrated how useless such theories were.
   c. built a bridge from Freud to more modern theories.
   d. developed a theory that most people believe today.

10.7 Rogers postulated that changing our perceptions of reality so that they are consistent with our self-concept is an example of the defense of
   a. adjustment.
   b. distortion.
   c. denial.
   d. contagion.

10.8 Allport's concept where patterns of behavior initially acquired under one set of circumstances necessary to satisfy one set of behavior and then later performed for very different reasons or motives is called
   a. functional autonomy.
   b. self-actualization.
   c. unconditional positive regard.
   d. ideal self.

10.9 Cattell used factor analysis techniques to identify _____ basic personality dimensions.
   a. 4
   b. 8
   c. 16
   d. 32

10.10 Which of the following is not one of the five key dimensions of personality identified by recent research?
   a. extraversion
   b. agreeableness
   c. intelligence
   d. conscientiousness

10.11 One important criticism of the trait approach to personality is that it does not
   a. explain how traits influence behavior.
   b. predict how a specific person will behave.
   c. define what a personality trait is.
   d. show how to measure the basic traits.

10.12 Your textbook speculates that the unique combination of high _____ combined with low _____ set the stage for Ms. McColm's lawsuits.
   a. extraversion and intelligence, conscientiousness and openness to experience
   b. intelligence and acting skill, agreeableness and emotional stability
   c. agreeableness and emotional stability, intelligence and acting skill
   d. conscientiousness and openness to experience, extraversion and intelligence

10.13 In Bandura's theory, our perceived ability to carry out a desired action is called
   a. self-reinforcement.
   b. self-efficacy.
   c. self-regulation.
   d. self-esteem.

10.14 One of the major advantages of the MCMI when compared to other personality inventories is that it allows the tester to
   a. screen people for specific psychological disorders.
   b. determine who will work best at a given job.
   c. predict which therapy will work best for a patient.
   d. exercise considerable judgment in scoring the results.

10.15 On which of these skills do high self-monitors perform better than other people?
   a. Maintaining consistent behavior across situations.
   b. Judging how others will react to their actions.
   c. Setting their own goals and rewarding their own behavior.
   d. Expressing their true attitudes in every situation.

PRACTICE TESTS

Practice Test 2

10.1 Freud postulated that the personality consisted of the following three parts - the
  a. conative, affective, and cognitive.
  b. conscious, preconscious, and unconscious.
  c. id, ego, and superego.
  d. anima, animus, and shadow.

10.2 According to Freud, the ego protects against anxiety by using
  a. fixation.
  b. fantasy.
  c. conflict.
  d. defense mechanisms.

10.3 According to Freud, adult personality is determined by what happens during
  a. adulthood.
  b. the prenatal period.
  c. infancy.
  d. the psychosexual stages.

10.4 The instinctual life force that energizes the id is known as
  a. the libido.
  b. the subconscious.
  c. the archetype.
  d. the self-concept.

10.5 Research on the _____, when combined with other research results lends support for the idea that our behavior is sometimes influenced by thoughts, ideas, or feelings we can't recognize – the unconscious, according to Freud.
  a. processes of hypnotism
  b. unconscious repeating of words
  c. subliminal conditioning of attitudes
  d. spontaneous remission of emotions.

10.6 One of the major features of Jung's theory was the _____, the inherited manifestations of the collective unconscious that shape our perceptions of the external world.
  a. shadow
  b. self-concept
  c. real-ideal discrepancy
  d. archetype

10.7 Masculine side of females is to feminine side of males as
  a. introvert is to extrovert.
  b. inferiority is to superiority.
  c. libido is to thanatos.
  d. animus is to anima.

10.8 According to Adler, personality development stemmed primarily from
  a. striving for superiority.
  b. achieving equality.
  c. avoidance of basic anxiety.
  d. maintaining self-esteem.

10.9 In Rogers' theory, the self-concept can become badly distorted due to parents' use of
  a. unconditional positive regard.
  b. conditional positive regard.
  c. negative reinforcement.
  d. avoidance-avoidance conflicts.

10.10 One major criticism about humanistic theories is that
   a. there is a lack of conceptualization.
   b. the concepts are loosely defined.
   c. the origins are not clear.
   d. there is an emphasis on determinism.

10.11 According to Allport, Hitler's drive for domination would be a
   a. cardinal trait.
   b. central trait.
   c. autonomous trait.
   d. functional trait.

10.12 Ralph tends to be nervous, anxious about almost every situation, and highly excitable. Ralph would probably be classified as low on the _____ dimension of the "Big Five" trait theory.
   a. extraversion
   b. agreeableness
   c. conscientiousness
   d. emotional stability

10.13 One important criticism of the trait approach to personality is that it does not
   a. explain how traits influence behavior.
   b. predict how a specific person will behave.
   c. define what a personality trait is.
   d. show how to measure the basis traits.

10.14 One key strength of the learning approach to personality is that it agrees with which of these basic principles of psychology?
   a. All human beings are basically evil.
   b. All human beings are basically good.
   c. Behaviors are acquired through learning.
   d. There are a few basic traits of personality.

10.15 Which of the following is not a characteristic of high sensation seekers?
   a. more likely to engage in high risk sports
   b. more likely to engage in substance abuse
   c. less likely to withstand stress
   d. operate best at high level of stress

PRACTICE TESTS

Chapter 11 - Health, Stress, and Coping

Practice Test 1

11.3 The field that combines behavioral and biomedical knowledge for the prevention and treatment of medical disorders is
   a. physiological psychology.
   b. behavioral medicine.
   c. bio-behaviorism.
   d. neuroscience.

11.2 The Alameda County, California study in which the relationship between healthy lifestyles and incidence of death was investigated is one of the best examples of a/an
   a. longitudinal study.
   b. epidemiological study.
   c. cross-sectional study.
   d. lifestyle study.

11.3 The stage of the GAS when arousal is lowered as the body copes with the stressor is the
   a. coping stage.
   b. resistance stage.
   c. alarm stage.
   d. exhaustion stage.

11.4 According to the cognitive appraisal perspective, stress occurs when people
   a. are in the coping stage.
   b. are goal oriented.
   c. are in the resistance stage.
   d. feel unable to cope with demands.

11.5 Being asked to do too many things in a short period of time is called work
   a. conflict.
   b. overload.
   c. underload.
   d. incompatibility.

11.6 The negative effects of stress on health appears to result from its interference in the _____ system.
   a. nervous
   b. endocrine
   c. cardiovascular
   d. immune

11.7 Optimists tend to be more stress-resistant than pessimists. This may be due to optimists using _____ coping.
   a. problem-focused
   b. emotion-focused
   c. denial
   d. psychological modification

11.8 Which is true of hardy individuals? They
   a. are not stress resistant.
   b. see change as a challenge.
   c. do not have a sense of control.
   d. have a low level of commitment.

11.9 Ford and colleagues (1996), in a study on communication between physicians and new cancer patients, found that the interactions tended to be _____ rather than _____.
    a. cooperative, directive
    b. psychological-focused, medical-focused
    c. clinician-dominated, patient-centered
    d. patient-centered, clinician-dominated

11.10 Which of the following is false?
    a. Individuals who have experienced stressful life events tend to have a high incidence of illness.
    b. Optimists are more resistant to stress than pessimists.
    c. Persons who have few distractions in their lives are more likely to notice symptoms than those who have many distractions.
    d. Smoking does not appear to be influenced by psychosocial factors.

11.11 What factor has been shown to increase a nonsmoking woman's chance of developing lung cancer?
    a. Moderate drinking
    b. Eating a high-fat diet
    c. Sun exposure
    d. Passive smoking

11.12 The reduction of the immune system's ability to defend itself against the introduction of any foreign matter is called
    a. acquired immune deficiency syndrome.
    b. HIV.
    c. stress exhaustion.
    d. antibody deficiencies.

11.13 The chances of _____ transmission of HIV are much greater than _____ transmission.
    a. different ethnic, same ethnic
    b. different culture, same culture
    c. male-to-female, female-to-male
    d. female-to-male, male-to-female

11.14 Which of the following can increase adherence to an exercise program?
    a. arranging cues to signal exercise, for example, working out in the same location
    b. arranging cues that allow you to be alone and away from a social support network
    c. minimizing consequences that can lead to rewards
    d. recognizing the importance of exercise.

11.15 Prevention strategies that are designed to increase early detection are called
    a. preliminary.
    b. tertiary.
    c. primary.
    d. secondary.

PRACTICE TESTS

43

Practice Test 2

11.1 Health psychology reflects the view that _____ contribute significantly to the onset or prevention of illness.
- a. self-concept, self-efficacy, and self-esteem
- b. anima, animas, and shadow
- c. beliefs, attitudes, and behaviors
- d. conscious, preconscious, and unconscious

11.2 Research indicates that many of the major causes of death are related to the _____ of the individual.
- a. psychological hardiness
- b. environment stressors
- c. genetic structure
- d. lifestyle

11.3 Large-scale studies that attempt to identify risk factors that predict the development of certain diseases are known as
- a. longitudinal studies.
- b. epidemiological studies.
- c. categorization studies.
- d. psychometric studies.

11.4 Which of the following is not typical of stressful events?
- a. a state of overload, feeling that you can not adapt to the stress
- b. evoking of incompatible tendencies
- c. the belief that the stress is beyond our limits of control
- d. a predictable situation for most individuals

11.5 Holmes and Rahe (1967) found a _____ correlation between the number of stress points on their scale and the likelihood of becoming seriously ill.
- a. selective
- b. positive
- c. negative
- d. neutral

11.6 In general, the greater the number of stressful life events for an individual, the greater the likelihood that the person's _____ will be negatively affected.
- a. health
- b. emotions
- c. cognitions
- d. dissonance

11.7 If employees feel that their performance appraisals are fair, employee _____ tends to be low.
- a. activity
- b. reaction
- c. stress
- d. accessibility

11.8 Victims of burnout frequently
- a. change jobs or withdraw psychologically by simply passing time until retirement.
- b. remain helpless and suffer several bouts of depression.
- c. initiate the resistance stage of the stress reactions.
- d. seek out social support.

11.9 One of the strategies that _____ might use to cope with stress is suppressing competing activities.
- a. a pessimist
- b. an idealist
- c. a realist
- d. an optimist

11.10 Research has shown that we are _____ to notice symptoms when there are _____.
a. least likely, few causes
b. most likely, few distractions
c. most likely, many distractions
d. least likely, many causes

11.11 In 1981, when physicians talked to their patients, they were more likely to focus on
a. affective issues.
b. psychological issues.
c. medical issues.
d. cognitive issues.

11.12 Lifestyle features that affect our chances of becoming ill are termed _____ factors.
a. risk
b. carcinogen
c. punishment
d. individual

11.13 The theory that suggests that the motivation for maintaining health-promoting behaviors depends upon the type of motivation behind the behaviors is called
a. intrinsic motivation theory.
b. extrinsic motivation theory.
c. self-determination theory.
d. cognitive-motivation theory.

11.14 A smoker who also drinks alcohol regularly is likely to show
a. a reduced risk of cancer.
b. an increased risk of cancer.
c. little or no cognitive impairment.
d. extreme risks of birth defects.

11.15 Researchers speculate that _____ may be related to increased risk of heart attack in Type A individuals.
a. impatience
b. competitiveness
c. hostility
d. cynical hostility

PRACTICE TESTS

Chapter 12 - Psychological Disorders: Their Nature and Causes

Practice Test 1

12.1 A young woman who displayed her ankles in public was once considered wanton and sexually promiscuous. The fact that this is no longer true in the U.S. demonstrates that
 a. distressing behavior is not always abnormal.
 b. social definitions of abnormality change over time.
 c. society no longer labels certain actions as unacceptable.
 d. people are more sexually active than they once were.

12.2 Which of Freud's views is most instrumental today in understanding abnormal behavior?
 a. his suggestion that the ego demands immediate gratification
 b. his suggestion that mental patients should be treated humanely
 c. his suggestion that psychological disorders are types of mental illnesses
 d. his suggestion that unconscious thoughts or impulses play a role in abnormal behavior

12.3 There are two major categories of mood disorders. They are _____ and _____ disorders.
 a. bipolar; euphoric
 b. euphoric; dysphoric
 c. bipolar; unipolar
 d. depressive; bipolar

12.4 For several weeks, Lisa has been extremely unhappy. She has difficulty getting out of bed and feels worthless. She is most likely suffering from
 a. major depression.
 b. a personality disorder.
 c. bipolar mood disorder.
 d. agoraphobia.

12.5 Disorders in which an individual experiences intense anxiety toward specific objects or situations are called
 a. personality fears.
 b. antisocial personality disorders.
 c. fugue.
 d. phobias.

12.6 The disorder that involves anxieties that involve repetitive behaviors is called
 a. obsessive-compulsive.
 b. phobia.
 c. panic.
 d. generalized anxiety.

12.7 People who exhibit physical symptoms that have no underlying physical cause have _____ disorders.
 a. anxiety
 b. organic
 c. dissociative
 d. somatoform

12.8 Lengthy losses of memory are known as _____ disorders.
 a. anxiety
 b. personality
 c. dissociative
 d. cognitive

12.9 When a person appears to have two or more distinct personalities, that person is said to have which disorder?
   a. schizophrenic disorder.
   b. somatoform disorder.
   c. conversion disorder.
   d. dissociative identity disorder.

12.10 The disorder in which individuals report sexual urges and fantasies involving sexual activity with children usually younger than thirteen is referred to as
   a. voyeurism.
   b. pedophilia.
   c. fetishism.
   d. orgasm disorder.

12.11 When individuals are very fearful of gaining weight and fail to maintain a normal body weight, they have
   a. paraphilia nervosa.
   b. anorexia nervosa.
   c. bulimia nervosa.
   d. neologism nervosa.

12.12 A schizoid personality disorder is characterized by
   a. physical symptoms that have no underlying cause.
   b. a desire to alter primary and secondary sex characteristics.
   c. social detachment and emotional coldness.
   d. multiple personalities.

12.13 The term that refers to the jumbled and meaningless speech patterns shown by schizophrenics who jump from one topic to the next with no organization is
   a. delusion.
   b. hallucination.
   c. paraphilia.
   d. word salad.

12.14 When schizophrenics believe they are under the control of outside forces they have delusions of
   a. grandeur.
   b. control.
   c. persecution.
   d. power.

12.15 Which of the following statements about suicide is not true?
   a. The majority of persons who commit suicide have told others about their intentions.
   b. If you think someone is suicidal, bringing up the topic and talking to them about it can help.
   c. Someone who is contemplating suicide should be left alone to think through the issues.
   d. Giving away valued possessions and starting to come out of a deep depression are associated with suicide attempts.

PRACTICE TESTS

Practice Test 2

12.1 One of the physicians from the 1700s who is known for removing the chains from patients with psychological disorders is
   a. Wilhelm Wundt.
   b. Sigmund Freud.
   c. Philippe Pinel.
   d. Alfred Binet.

12.2 A system for diagnosing psychological disorders is found in the
   a. WAIS-III
   b. DSM-IV.
   c. NEO-II.
   d. 16 PF

12.3 Examples such as depression and bipolar disorders would be put in the diagnostic category of
   a. personality disorders.
   b. factitious disorders.
   c. mood disorders.
   d. schizophrenia.

12.4 Which of the following statements does not accurately describe the use of the DSM-IV?
   a. It provides a useful tool for explaining abnormal behavior.
   b. It provides a useful tool for describing abnormal behavior.
   c. It classifies disorders along five axes.
   d. Its use may be subject to bias in making clinical judgments about the severity or presence of psychological disorders.

12.5 Which of these is a list of symptoms associated with major depressive disorder?
   a. tension, panic attacks, withdrawal, and avoidance
   b. sadness, loss of appetite, insomnia, and guilt
   c. delusions, hallucinations, catatonia, and tension
   d. excessive emotion and attention-getting behavior

12.6 One of the warning signs for the onset of depression is
   a. significant loss of hair.
   b. inability to engage in altruistic behavior.
   c. lack of physical movement.
   d. inability to concentrate.

12.7 When asked to describe themselves, depressed people are more likely to
   a. give negative ratings to themselves.
   b. give negative ratings to others.
   c. give neutral ratings themselves.
   d. give positive ratings and to themselves.

12.8 Individuals suffering from depression seem to possess
   a. negative self-schemas.
   b. expressive facetiousness.
   c. negative dissonance.
   d. covert emotionality.

12.9 In the study by Terry and colleagues (1996) on postpartum depression, the results indicated that there was a _____ correlation between feelings of personal control and experienced depression.
 a. curvilinear
 b. positive
 c. neutral
 d. negative

12.10 Suicide is more often attempted by _____. Ending of one's life through suicide is more often completed by _____.
 a. men; men
 b. women; men
 c. women; women
 d. men; women

12.11 A disorder in which an individual experiences high levels of physiological arousal coupled with intense fear of losing control is called
 a. phobia.
 b. schizophrenia.
 c. mood disorder.
 d. panic attack disorder.

12.12 Ralph was going to work one morning, and instead of turning right on Oak Street, he turned left and was not heard of for the next eight years until he was seen with at a hospital with a different wife and two children. He did not recall his previous life, and was diagnosed as having
 a. schizophrenia.
 b. panic disorder.
 c. dissociative fugue.
 d. manic-depressive disorder.

12.13 An individual who has sexual urges involving exposing his or her genitals to an unsuspecting stranger would be diagnosed as having
 a. masochism.
 b. exhibitionism.
 c. voyeurism.
 d. fetishism

12.14 A person with _____ believes that he or she is being plotted against, spied on, or mistreated in some way.
 a. delusions of control
 b. delusions of grandeur
 c. delusions of persecution
 d. delusions of maltreatment

12.15 Which of these is not a pattern of family interaction that has been claimed to cause schizophrenia?
 a. Extremely high levels of conflict between the parents.
 b. One or both parents sexually abuse the child.
 c. All social power in the family rests with one parent.
 d. Child is placed in a double bind.

PRACTICE TESTS

Chapter 13 - Therapy: Diminishing the Pain of Psychological Disorders

Practice Test 1

13.1 Procedures in which a trained person establishes a special relationship with an individual seeking help in order to remove or modify existing symptoms, change disturbed patterns of behavior, and promote personal growth are called
   a. behavioral medicine.
   b. psychotherapies.
   c. psychobiological therapies.
   d. psychopharmacological therapies.

13.2 Freud suggested that psychological disorders stem from _____ of id impulses.
   a. interpretation
   b. repression
   c. transference
   d. abreaction

13.3 Which of the following is not one of the primary features of client-centered therapy?
   a. unconditional acceptance
   b. interpretation of dreams
   c. accurate reflection of clients' feelings
   d. emphatic understanding

13.4 In a token economy, the tokens (poker chips, gold stars, etc.) function to reinforce desired behaviors because
   a. they have special, individual meaning for the client.
   b. they can be used to buy other reinforcements (treats).
   c. they are able to serve as a conditioned stimulus.
   d. they are able to serve as an unconditioned stimulus.

13.5 The main function of rational-emotive therapy is to persuade people to
   a. recognize their own irrational beliefs and assumptions.
   b. confront the people who have let them down in life.
   c. get in touch with feelings they are trying to deny.
   d. reach their full potential as human beings.

13.6 A type of therapy that involves several people all meeting together to receive psychological help is called
   a. psychoanalysis.
   b. group therapy.
   c. humanistic therapy.
   d. intermittent therapy.

13.7 A basic assumption of self-help groups is that when you are facing a problem in your life
   a. it is generally caused by illogical thought processes that need to change.
   b. it is important to understand the basic cause of your problem from your past.
   c. you will need to find a caring, trained professional to help you deal with it.
   d. no professional can help as much as someone who has faced the same problem.

13.8 In general, the research that has been performed to evaluate the success of family therapy has led to the conclusion that after participating in family therapy
   a. family members relate to each other better.
   b. children become more intelligent.
   c. unconscious urges are weaker.
   d. people have more accurate self-concepts.

13.9 The *Consumer Reports* study on the effectiveness of therapy found that
   a. the shorter the therapy sessions, the greater the improvement.
   b. the more education provided about the disorder, the greater the improvement.
   c. the longer therapy continued, the greater the improvement.
   d. the more specific the disorder, the greater the improvement.

13.10 Which of these is not a likely reason for therapy to be less effective for people of varying cultural and ethnic backgrounds?
   a. Therapists might have difficulty communicating with people very different from themselves.
   b. Therapies were originally developed for middle-class people of European descent.
   c. People of different racial backgrounds show different patterns of brain chemistry.
   d. Therapists might be subject to subtle or unconscious forms of cultural bias.

13.11 Which of the following is true of antipsychotic drugs?
   a. They do seem to relieve major symptoms of schizophrenia.
   b. They do seem to eliminate the causes that underlie schizophrenia.
   c. They are not often associated with side-effects.
   d. They are sometimes known as minor tranquilizers.

13.12 The neurotransmitter effects most likely to be modified by the use of antidepressant drugs are those of
   a. dopamine and acetylcholine.
   b. serotonin and norepinephrine.
   c. substance P and glycine.
   d. GABA and endorphins.

13.13 Electroconvulsive therapy should be used with caution. However, it appears to be effective with severe
   a. drug addictions.
   b. depression.
   c. dissociative disorders.
   d. alcohol addictions.

13.14 Which of the following were designed to deliver emergency services for individuals suffering from psychological problems?
   a. state mental institutions
   b. private mental hospitals
   c. community mental health centers
   d. milieu therapy centers

13.15 A general guideline used in determining when you should expect to see some progress during therapy is about
   a. three weeks.
   b. three months.
   c. ten to fourteen days.
   d. six months.

PRACTICE TESTS

Practice Test 2

13.1 Which of the following is not one of the characteristics of psychoanalysis?
   a. empathy
   b. free association
   c. transference
   d. abreaction

13.2 Carl Rogers developed the humanistic approach of
   a. conditions of worth therapy.
   b. Gestalt therapy.
   c. client-centered therapy.
   d. self-actualization theory.

13.3 Which of the following is not one of the assumptions of humanistic therapies?
   a. People have control over their own behavior.
   b. Flaws in self-concept produce psychological distress.
   c. People have the ability to make choices.
   d. The therapist must force repressed urges from patients.

13.4 Therapies that do not concentrate on hidden impulses, conflicts, etc., but instead concentrate on current behavior are known as
   a. humanistic therapies.
   b. behavior therapies.
   c. currency therapies.
   d. psychodynamic therapies.

13.5 The individual who developed Rational-Emotive Therapy was
   a. Alfred Binet.
   b. Albert Bandura.
   c. Alfred Adler.
   d. Albert Ellis.

13.6 Encounter groups and sensitivity-training groups are a product of
   a. behavioral group therapies.
   b. humanistic group therapies.
   c. psychodynamic group therapies.
   d. behavioral individual therapies.

13.7 Family Systems Therapy treats the family as a _____ in which each member as a major role.
   a. divergent system
   b. coactive system
   c. dynamic system
   d. cooperative system

13.8 Currently, about _____ of the population in the United States have had contact with a psychotherapist.
   a. 10%
   b. 20%
   c. 30%
   d. 40%

13.9 In evaluating psychotherapy, _____ adhere to scientific method guidelines, while _____ adhere to conditions of actual practice.
   a. effectiveness studies, efficacy studies
   b. elicitation studies, efficacy studies
   c. efficacy studies, elicitation studies
   d. efficacy studies, effectiveness studies

13.10 Which of the following is not one of the features held in common by the different therapies?
a. therapeutic alliance
b. psychodrama
c. special kind of setting
d. suggestion of specific actions in order to cope with problems

13.11 If a psychological problem is causing you _____, you should consider seeing a therapist.
a. extended social enhancement
b. fleeting, yet recurrent cognition
c. serious emotional discomfort
d. limited functional autonomy

13.12 At the current time, psychologists do not have
a. professional restrictions.
b. ethical limitations.
c. prescription privileges.
d. therapy guidelines.

13.13 So many drugs have been developed in recent years that are effective in treating psychological disorders that some say psychology has experienced
a. a drug enhanced revolution.
b. a philological revolution.
c. a pharmacological revolution.
d. a prescription revolution

13.14 The condition called tardive dyskinesia often occurs among patients who are maintained on _____ drugs.
a. antidepressant
b. antipsychotic
c. antimania
d. antianxiety

13.15 The drug that has been found to be effective in treating bipolar disorders is called
a. Halium.
b. Librium.
c. Valium.
d. Lithium.

PRACTICE TESTS

53

Chapter 14 - Social Thought and Social Behavior

Practice Test 1

14.1   According to Kelley, if a person reacts the same way to a given stimulus or situation on different occasions (i.e., across time), he/she exhibits
   a. low distinctiveness.
   b. high consistency.
   c. high consensus.
   d. low covariation.

14.2   The fundamental attribution error is the tendency to explain the behavior of others in terms of _____ causes.
   a. internal
   b. external
   c. stable
   d. unstable

14.3   The tendency to interpret the causes of our positive behavior as a result of an internal cause is the
   a. fundamental attribution error.
   b. basis of most gender differences.
   c. illusory correlation.
   d. self-serving bias.

14.4   An area of study concerned with understanding the processes through which we interpret, analyze, and thus use social information is called
   a. social attribution.
   b. social cognition.
   c. cognitive perspective.
   d. cognitive dissonance.

14.5   The principle of _____ implies that things that resemble one another share common properties.
   a. proximity
   b. contagion
   c. similarity
   d. continuity

14.6   The notion that our attitudes are formed on the basis of rewards delivered by our parents for expressing the "correct view" is based on
   a. social contagion.
   b. cognitive dissonance.
   c. operant conditioning.
   d. classical conditioning.

14.7   The central route to persuasion refers to
   a. the careful processing of arguments.
   b. the impact of persuasion cues on attitude change.
   c. attitude change that occurs because individuals recognize inconsistencies between their attitudes and their behavior.
   d. persuasion induced by fear.

14.8   One way of reducing the unpleasant feelings associated with dissonance is to
   a. deny that we have these unpleasant feelings.
   b. evaluate the information given us when we formed the attitude.
   c. confirm our feelings with someone else who has gone through this same situation.
   d. acquire new information that supports our attitude or behavior.

14.9 Recent research indicates that we can sometimes change our attitudes by doing or saying things
   a. out of character.
   b. in line with what we believe.
   c. we want to happen.
   d. we want others to do.

14.10 The view of prejudice that suggests that prejudice stems from competition between social groups over valued commodities or opportunities is the
   a. realistic conflict theory.
   b. cognitive dissonance theory.
   c. social learning theory.
   d. social categorization theory.

14.11 Which of these situations represents intergroup contact that might actually increase prejudice between the groups?
   a. Providing informal, one-to-one contact.
   b. Having the groups compete for prizes.
   c. Giving the groups equal status in the situation.
   d. Creating norms that support group equality.

14.12 Lisa is going for an interview for a desirable job. She puts on a powerful perfume, makes very flattering comments to the interviewer, and talks as if she knows a lot about the company. These compliance tactics
   a. will help her in her relationship with the interviewer.
   b. will be very successful for her.
   c. will more than likely backfire on her.
   d. will be powerful enough to make a positive impression.

14.13 The foot-in-the-door technique seems to be effective because people want to be
   a. consistent.
   b. dissonant.
   c. self-assured.
   d. self-confident.

14.14 An important factor in getting participants to obey in the obedience studies is that the person in authority relieves the participant of
   a. responsibility.
   b. emotion.
   c. awareness.
   d. cognition.

14.15 According to evolutionary theory, _____ enhances the tendency to engage in sexual intercourse and to commitment to provide long term child care.
   a. lust
   b. love
   c. cognition
   d. emotion

PRACTICE TESTS

Practice Test 2

14.1 According to Kelley, we tend to attribute behavior to external causes if consistency is _____, distinctiveness is _____, and consensus is _____.
 a. high; low; low
 b. high; high; high
 c. low; low; low
 d. low; high; high

14.2 The research by Bell and colleagues (1994) found that males and females attributed _____ blame to the victim of a date rape than to the victim of a stranger rape.
 a. less
 b. more
 c. equal
 d. social

14.3 The tendency to overestimate the extent to which we are similar to others is the _____ effect.
 a. false consensus
 b. priming
 c. illusory correlation
 d. self-serving bias

14.4 If someone talks about "What might have been." when talking about a situation, that person is engaging in
 a. cognitive dissonance.
 b. self-deception.
 c. self-handicapping.
 d. counterfactual thinking.

14.5 The _____ of attitude change concentrates on the question of what cognitive process are involved in determining attitude change.
 a. traditional approach
 b. cognitive dissonance interpretation
 c. cognitive perspective
 d. persuasion model

14.6 The Fantasy Man was successful in his endeavors because of his ability of
 a. persuasion.
 b. evaluation.
 c. equilibration.
 d. stereotyping.

14.7 There is a _____ correlation between strength of dissonance and amount of attitude change.
 a. equal
 b. neutral
 c. negative
 d. positive

14.8 This view of prejudice emphasizes the role of stereotypes.
 a. realistic conflict
 b. social categorization
 c. social learning
 d. cognitive

14.9 Norms that specify what should be done are called
   a. realistic norms.
   b. disjunctive norms.
   c. injunctive norms.
   d. descriptive norms.

14.10 Lisa is trying to get her friend to donate money to a worthy cause. Because Lisa is asking her friend to donate, she is using the _____ of friendship to influence her friend.
   a. obedience principle
   b. compliance principle
   c. conformity principle
   d. dissonance principle

14.11 In the door-in-the-face technique, the first request is a _____ one and the second request is a _____ one.
   a. large; small
   b. small; large
   c. large; large
   d. small; moderate

14.12 In Milgram's study on obedience, he found that approximately _____ of the participants were fully obedient.
   a. 35%
   b. 65%
   c. 75%
   d. 85%

14.13 Ralph helped Lisa fix the tire on her car one evening in the rain, even thought Lisa did not ask him. Ralph was engaging in
   a. compliance behavior.
   b. conformity behavior.
   c. prosocial behavior.
   d. manipulative behavior.

14.14 The extent to which we like or dislike other persons is called
   a. affective coherence.
   b. interpersonal attraction.
   c. prosocial behavior.
   d. empathy behavior.

14.15 The _____ of attraction is that choosing attractive mates increases the probability of contributing our genes to the next generation.
   a. genetic explanation
   b. physique explanation
   c. proximity explanation
   d. evolutionary perspective

PRACTICE TESTS

Answer Keys

Chapter 1: Practice Test 1

QUESTION	ANSWER	PAGE NUMBER
1.1	d	4
1.2	c	4
1.3	d	7
1.4	c	9
1.5	c	13
1.6	a	14
1.7	b	15
1.8	d	17
1.9	c	21
1.10	a	21
1.11	a	22
1.12	c	25
1.13	b	29
1.14	d	30
1.15	c	32

Chapter 1: Practice Test 2

QUESTION	ANSWER	PAGE NUMBER
1.1	d	4
1.2	a	5
1.3	b	5
1.4	b	6
1.5	c	11
1.6	b	14
1.7	d	22
1.8	a	25
1.9	b	25
1.10	b	27
1.11	c	27
1.12	a	30
1.13	c	30
1.14	a	32
1.15	d	34

BARON - ESSENTIALS OF PSYCHOLOGY (2ND Edition)

Answer Keys

Chapter 2: Practice Test 1

QUESTION	ANSWER	PAGE NUMBER
2.1	c	41
2.2	b	42
2.3	d	42
2.4	a	43
2.5	b	45
2.6	b	47
2.7	d	52
2.8	d	54
2.9	c	58
2.10	d	60
2.11	a	60
2.12	b	64
2.13	d	67
2.14	c	69
2.15	b	70

Chapter 2: Practice Test 2

QUESTION	ANSWER	PAGE NUMBER
2.1	a	41
2.2	b	43
2.3	c	44
2.4	d	46
2.5	c	51
2.6	d	52
2.7	d	56
2.8	b	57
2.9	b	59
2.10	b	61
2.11	d	63
2.12	c	65
2.13	c	70
2.14	a	72
2.15	b	74

PRACTICE TESTS

Answer Keys

Chapter 3: Practice Test 1

QUESTION	ANSWER	PAGE NUMBER
3.1	b	80
3.2	c	81
3.3	a	84
3.4	c	87
3.5	b	89
3.6	a	94
3.7	c	97
3.8	b	100
3.9	c	102
3.10	d	108
3.11	b	110
3.12	d	113
3.13	c	116
3.14	a	118
3.15	c	120

Chapter 3: Practice Test 2

QUESTION	ANSWER	PAGE NUMBER
3.1	d	80
3.2	c	82
3.3	b	82
3.4	a	86
3.5	b	88
3.6	d	92
3.7	c	95
3.8	a	96
3.9	b	99
3.10	a	105
3.11	b	105
3.12	c	109
3.13	b	114
3.14	c	115
3.15	d	117

BARON - ESSENTIALS OF PSYCHOLOGY (2ND Edition)

Answer Keys

Chapter 4: Practice Test 1

QUESTION	ANSWER	PAGE NUMBER
4.1	d	127
4.2	d	133
4.3	d	135
4.4	d	136
4.5	b	139
4.6	b	141
4.7	a	142
4.8	b	143
4.9	a	146
4.10	b	151
4.11	a	152
4.12	b	152
4.13	d	155
4.14	d	156
4.15	b	158

Chapter 4: Practice Test 2

QUESTION	ANSWER	PAGE NUMBER
4.1	b	131
4.2	c	133
4.3	a	135
4.4	b	135
4.5	c	137
4.6	d	138
4.7	d	141
4.8	b	145
4.9	c	148
4.10	a	151
4.11	d	153
4.12	b	154
4.13	c	156
4.14	a	157
4.15	d	158

PRACTICE TESTS

Answer Keys

Chapter 5: Practice Test 1

QUESTION	ANSWER	PAGE NUMBER
5.1	d	164
5.2	b	166
5.3	a	167
5.4	b	169
5.5	c	169
5.6	c	173
5.7	d	174
5.8	b	177
5.9	a	179
5.10	b	182
5.11	b	183
5.12	a	186
5.13	a	188
5.14	c	195
5.15	c	199

Chapter 5: Practice Test 2

QUESTION	ANSWER	PAGE NUMBER
5.1	b	165
5.2	c	167
5.3	d	168
5.4	a	170
5.5	b	173
5.6	c	175
5.7	d	178
5.8	b	179
5.9	b	180
5.10	d	183
5.11	d	184
5.12	b	184
5.13	a	187
5.14	c	190
5.15	c	192

BARON - ESSENTIALS OF PSYCHOLOGY (2ND Edition)

Answer Keys

Chapter 6: Practice Test 1

QUESTION	ANSWER	PAGE NUMBER
6.1	c	207
6.2	c	209
6.3	b	213
6.4	a	215
6.5	b	216
6.6	c	221
6.7	b	223
6.8	b	224
6.9	c	227
6.10	c	227
6.11	b	228
6.12	b	234
6.13	a	235
6.14	c	236
6.15	c	239

Chapter 6: Practice Test 2

QUESTION	ANSWER	PAGE NUMBER
6.1	b	206
6.2	d	208
6.3	b	211
6.4	d	212
6.5	d	215
6.6	c	217
6.7	a	218
6.8	b	219
6.9	a	222
6.10	b	225
6.11	b	226
6.12	c	229
6.13	c	237
6.14	a	238
6.15	d	240

PRACTICE TESTS

Answer Keys

Chapter 7: Practice Test 1

QUESTION	ANSWER	PAGE NUMBER
7.1	d	246
7.2	d	248
7.3	a	249
7.4	c	253
7.5	d	256
7.6	a	263
7.7	c	266
7.8	a	269
7.9	b	270
7.10	d	272
7.11	b	276
7.12	d	277
7.13	c	280
7.14	a	282
7.15	b	286

Chapter 7: Practice Test 2

QUESTION	ANSWER	PAGE NUMBER
7.1	a	247
7.2	b	250
7.3	c	251
7.4	a	252
7.5	d	254
7.6	b	256
7.7	c	257
7.8	b	259
7.9	d	261
7.10	c	262
7.11	a	265
7.12	b	269
7.13	c	270
7.14	b	274
7.15	c	277

Answer Keys

Chapter 8: Practice Test 1

QUESTION	ANSWER	PAGE NUMBER
8.1	d	294
8.2	c	300
8.3	d	301
8.4	b	303
8.5	b	304
8.6	b	308
8.7	d	311
8.8	c	313
8.9	a	314
8.10	a	319
8.11	c	324
8.12	a	324
8.13	d	326
8.14	a	330
8.15	a	331

Chapter 8: Practice Test 2

QUESTION	ANSWER	PAGE NUMBER
8.1	b	295
8.2	a	296
8.3	c	298
8.4	d	299
8.5	a	301
8.6	c	301
8.7	d	304
8.8	b	306
8.9	b	308
8.10	d	316
8.11	d	321
8.12	c	322
8.13	b	324
8.14	d	326
8.15	a	329

PRACTICE TESTS

Answer Keys

Chapter 9: Practice Test 1

QUESTION	ANSWER	PAGE NUMBER
9.1	b	341
9.2	c	342
9.3	a	343
9.4	a	344
9.5	b	344
9.6	a	347
9.7	b	350
9.8	a	355
9.9	a	360
9.10	a	362
9.11	b	365
9.12	d	366
9.13	b	366
9.14	b	370
9.15	c	373

Chapter 9: Practice Test 2

QUESTION	ANSWER	PAGE NUMBER
9.1	b	340
9.2	c	342
9.3	d	343
9.4	c	344
9.5	b	344
9.6	c	348
9.7	b	351
9.8	d	357
9.9	c	360
9.10	b	360
9.11	a	362
9.12	b	364
9.13	d	365
9.14	b	369
9.15	c	371

Answer Keys

Chapter 10: Practice Test 1

QUESTION	ANSWER	PAGE NUMBER
10.1	c	381
10.2	b	383
10.3	d	383
10.4	d	385
10.5	b	387
10.6	c	389
10.7	b	390
10.8	d	394
10.9	c	394
10.10	c	395
10.11	a	396
10.12	b	398
10.13	b	400
10.14	a	404
10.15	b	407

Chapter 10: Practice Test 2

QUESTION	ANSWER	PAGE NUMBER
10.1	c	382
10.2	d	383
10.3	d	384
10.4	a	384
10.5	c	386
10.6	d	387
10.7	d	388
10.8	a	388
10.9	b	391
10.10	b	393
10.11	a	394
10.12	d	395
10.13	a	396
10.14	c	401
10.15	c	407

PRACTICE TESTS

Answer Keys

Chapter 11: Practice Test 1

QUESTION	ANSWER	PAGE NUMBER
11.1	b	416
11.2	b	418
11.3	b	419
11.4	d	420
11.5	b	424
11.6	d	426
11.7	a	429
11.8	b	430
11.9	c	433
11.10	d	435
11.11	d	436
11.12	a	440
11.13	c	443
11.14	a	448
11.15	d	448

Chapter 11: Practice Test 2

QUESTION	ANSWER	PAGE NUMBER
11.1	c	416
11.2	d	417
11.3	b	418
11.4	d	419
11.5	b	423
11.6	a	423
11.7	c	425
11.8	a	428
11.9	d	429
11.10	b	431
11.11	b	433
11.12	a	434
11.13	c	437
11.14	b	438
11.15	d	439

BARON - ESSENTIALS OF PSYCHOLOGY (2ND Edition)

Answer Keys

Chapter 12: Practice Test 1

QUESTION	ANSWER	PAGE NUMBER
12.1	b	458
12.2	d	461
12.3	d	466
12.4	a	466
12.5	d	473
12.6	a	475
12.7	d	477
12.8	c	478
12.9	d	479
12.10	b	481
12.11	b	483
12.12	c	485
12.13	d	488
12.14	b	488
12.15	c	492

Chapter 12: Practice Test 2

QUESTION	ANSWER	PAGE NUMBER
12.1	c	460
12.2	b	463
12.3	c	463
12.4	a	463
12.5	b	466
12.6	d	466
12.7	a	468
12.8	a	468
12.9	d	470
12.10	b	471
12.11	d	472
12.12	c	479
12.13	b	482
12.14	c	488
12.15	b	491

PRACTICE TESTS

Answer Keys

Chapter 13: Practice Test 1

QUESTION	ANSWER	PAGE NUMBER
13.1	b	498
13.2	b	499
13.3	b	502
13.4	b	504
13.5	a	506
13.6	b	509
13.7	d	510
13.8	a	514
13.9	c	517
13.10	c	521
13.11	a	523
13.12	b	523
13.13	b	526
13.14	c	527
13.15	b	529

Chapter 13: Practice Test 2

QUESTION	ANSWER	PAGE NUMBER
13.1	a	500
13.2	c	501
13.3	d	502
13.4	b	503
13.5	d	505
13.6	b	509
13.7	c	513
13.8	a	515
13.9	d	516
13.10	b	518
13.11	c	519
13.12	c	520
13.13	c	522
13.14	b	523
13.15	d	524

BARON - ESSENTIALS OF PSYCHOLOGY (2ND Edition)

Answer Keys

Chapter 14: Practice Test 1

QUESTION	ANSWER	PAGE NUMBER
14.1	b	535
14.2	a	536
14.3	d	536
14.4	b	537
14.5	c	540
14.6	c	543
14.7	a	545
14.8	d	547
14.9	b	548
14.10	a	550
14.11	b	552
14.12	c	556
14.13	a	556
14.14	a	558
14.15	b	566

Chapter 14: Practice Test 2

QUESTION	ANSWER	PAGE NUMBER
14.1	b	535
14.2	b	538
14.3	a	539
14.4	d	541
14.5	c	544
14.6	a	546
14.7	d	547
14.8	d	550
14.9	c	554
14.10	b	555
14.11	a	556
14.12	b	557
14.13	c	559
14.14	b	564
14.15	d	566